KS-3450

COLUMBIA

STEREO

GUITAR/VOCAL/CHORDS

brandi carlile
bear creek

EXCLUSIVELY DISTRIBUTED BY

HAL•LEONARD®

Transcribed by Dan Begelman

Printed in USA.

No part of this book shall be reproduced, arranged, adapted, recorded, publicly performed, stored in a retrieval system,
or transmitted by any means without written permission from the publisher. In order to comply with copyright laws, please apply
for such written permission and/or license by contacting the publisher at alfred.com/permissions.

ISBN-13: 978-0-7390-9106-7

CD Art Direction: Michelle Holme
Photography: Frank Ockenfels

HARD WAY HOME

Moderately in 2 ♩ = 94

Intro:

Words and Music by
TIM HANSEROTH, BRANDI CARLILE
and PHIL HANSEROTH

Verses 1, 2, & 3:

some-times lose my faith in luck, I don't know what I want to be___ when I___ grow up.___
2. *See additional lyrics*

___ I just count the rain,___ wear-ing the floor___ to the boards a-gain.___ I

wish I could find a soul to steal,___ I could be the en-gine, you could be___ the wheel.
3. *See additional lyrics*

___ And we could drive it home,___ and nev-er have to wor-ry a-bout be-ing a-lone.

Hard Way Home - 3 - 1

6

Verse 2:
Never did learn how to follow the rules,
I never was good at sleeping while the moon was full.
I'll just lie and burn,
Wreck my mind while the planet turns

I sometimes wish I could start again,
I'd try and do the right thing every now and then.
I'd step in line,
That's what I'd do if I could turn back time.
(To Pre-chorus:)

Verse 3:
I'll tell you how I want to live,
Forget about the take, forget about the give.
I want to leave this town,
Fake my death and never be found.
(To Pre-chorus:)

RAISE HELL

Words and Music by
BRANDI CARLILE and TIM HANSEROTH

Moderately in 2 ♩ = 110

Intro:

Verse 1:

Cont. rhy. simile

I've been down___ with a bro-ken heart___ since the day I learned to speak.

The dev-il gave___ me a crook-ed start___ when he gave me crook-ed

feet. But Ga-bri-el___ done came to me___ and kissed me in my

sleep. And I'll be sing-ing like an an-gel un-

Resume rhy. fig. simile

til I'm six feet___ deep.

2. I

*Chord is implied.

Raise Hell - 5 - 1

Verses 2 & 3:

found my - self an o - men and I tat - tooed on a sign.____

(3.) *See additional lyrics*

I set my mind to wan - der - ing____ and walk a bro - ken

line. You have a mind____ to keep me qui - et and

al - though you can try;____ bet - ter men have hit____

Resume rhy. fig. simile

____ their knees and big - ger men____ have____ died. I'm gon - na

𝄋 *Chorus:*

raise,_____ raise_____

____ hell._____ There's a

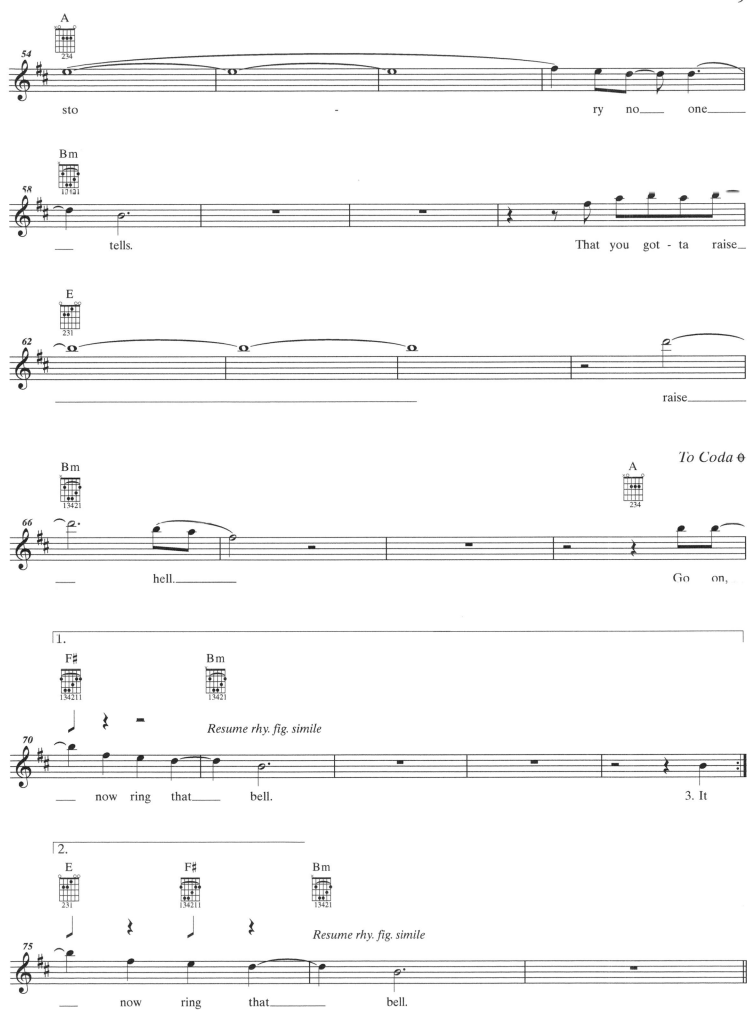

Instrumental:

Verse 4:

I dug a hole__ in - side my heart to put you in your grave.__

*Chords are implied.

Verse 3:
It came upon a lightning strike and eyes of bright clear blue.
I took that tie from around my neck and gave my heart to you.
I sent my love across the sea and though I didn't cry,
That voice will haunt my every dream until the day I die.
(To Chorus:)

SAVE PART OF YOURSELF

*Alternate tuning for Acous. Gtr. and Mandolin *(arr. for gtr.)*:

⑥ = D ③ = G
⑤ = G# ② = B
④ = D ① = D

Words and Music by
TIM HANSEROTH and BRANDI CARLILE

Moderately in 2 ♩ = 92

Intro:

1. The

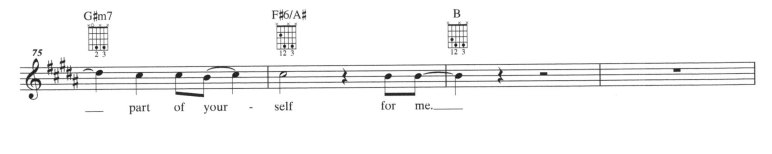

Verse 2:
I remember you and me lost and young and dumb and free,
Unaware of years to come.
Just a whisper in the dark on the pavement in the park,
You taught me how to love someone.
So save part of yourself for me.
Won't you save part of yourself for me.

Verse 3:
When we walk into the sun or burn below for what we've done,
Will you still call out for me.
Turn to light or fade to black
You don't look back, no, you don't look back,
At what you might not want to see.
But save part of yourself for me.
Won't you save part of yourself for me.

THAT WASN'T ME

Words and Music by
BRANDI CARLILE

*Recording sounds one whole step higher than written due to capo.

1. Hang on,___

Verse:

___ just hang on___ for a min-ute, I've got some-thing___ to say.

(2.) *See additional lyrics*

- ing___ you to move on___ or for-get it, but these are___ bet-ter days.___ To be wrong___

___ all a-long___ and ad-mit it is not a-maz-ing grace. But to be loved___

___ like a song___ you re-mem-ber e - ven when___ you've changed.___

___ Tell me...___ Did I go___

Chorus:

Bridge:

Chorus:

— my-self a bless-ing to ev-ery-one___ I meet?_____ When you fall___

___ I will get___ you___ on your feet._____ Do I spend

time with my fam-i-ly? Did it show_____ when I was weak?_____

___ When that's what you see,_____ that will be me.___

_____ That will be me._____ That will be

Freely

me._____ That will be me._____

Verse 2:
When you're lost you will toss every lucky coin you'll ever trust.
And you'll hide from your God like he ever turns his back on us.
Then you'll fall all the way to the bottom and land on your own knife.
And you'll learn who you are even if it doesn't take your life.
Tell me...
(To Chorus:)

KEEP YOUR HEART YOUNG

*To match recording, tune down 1/2 step:

⑥ = E♭   ③ = G♭
⑤ = A♭   ② = B♭
④ = D♭   ① = E♭

Words and Music by
TIM HANSEROTH and PHIL HANSEROTH

Keep Your Heart Young - 3 - 1

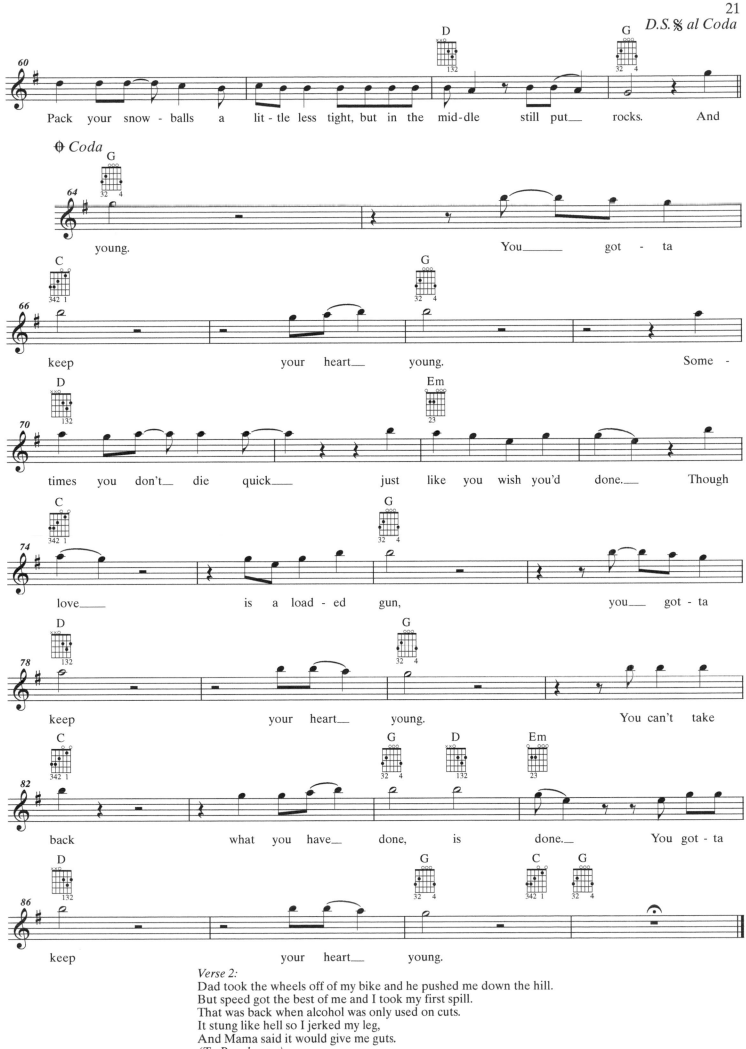

Verse 2:
Dad took the wheels off of my bike and he pushed me down the hill.
But speed got the best of me and I took my first spill.
That was back when alcohol was only used on cuts.
It stung like hell so I jerked my leg,
And Mama said it would give me guts.
(To Pre-chorus:)

100

Words and Music by
PHIL HANSEROTH and BRANDI CARLILE

*Recording sounds three whole steps higher than written due to capo..
TAB numbers and chord frames relative to capo.

Verse 1:

Cont. rhy. simile

blow-ing out the can - dles, and when peo-ple start to sing,___ I will

al - ways cross___ my fin - gers tight,_ I'll re-mem-ber ev-ery-thing. But I

Chorus 1:

al - ways make___ my wish - es for the same thing ev-ery-time.___ If I

live to be one hun - dred, if I ev - er get it right.

100 - 3 - 1

Instrumental:

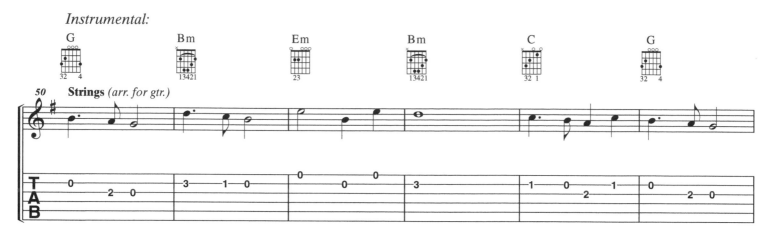

D.S. ℅ al Coda

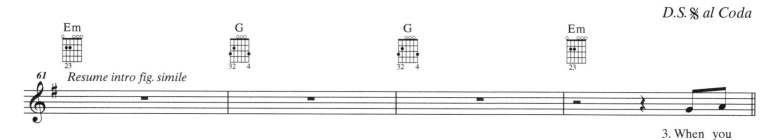

3. When you

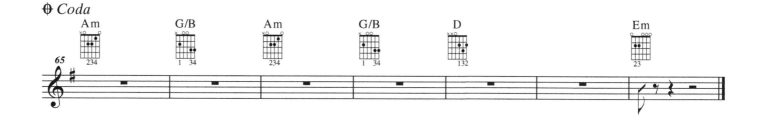

Verse 3:
When you close your eyes at night,
And you rise above your life,
Do you notice there an empty space where I wasn't by your side.

Chorus 3:
Because I always dream about you every time I close my eyes.
If I live to be 100,
Will I ever cross your mind?
I always make my wishes for the same thing every time.
If I live to be 100,
Will I ever cross your mind?

A PROMISE TO KEEP

Words and Music by
TIM HANSEROTH

Moderately in 2 ♩ = 98

Intro:

*Recording sounds two whole steps higher than written due to capo.
TAB numbers and chord frames relative to capo.

A Promise to Keep - 4 - 1

Outro:

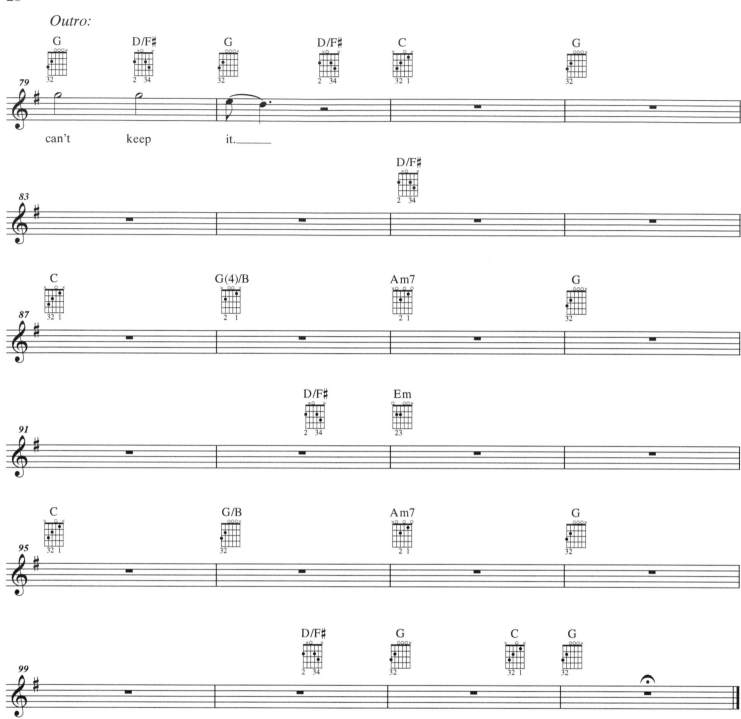

can't   keep   it.____

Verse 2:
I still lay on my side of the bed.
I dance alone when the last bottle's spent.
Memories like a river running through my head.
I'll have me an ocean before I'm dead.
(To Chorus:)

Verse 3:
I still whisper sweet words to you.
And when I'm busy with nothing to do,
I pray to God that my words ring true.
And that your words might reach me too.
(To Chorus:)

Verse 4:
My heart's in pieces so please understand.
I'm trying to jump but I've nowhere to land.
So give me your heart and I'll give you my hand,
And try as goddamned hard as I can.
(To Chorus:)

I'LL STILL BE THERE

Words and Music by
PHIL HANSEROTH and BRANDI CARLILE

Moderately ♩ = 112

Verses 1 & 2:

1. There nev-er was a bet-ter love to see the light of day.
(2.) *See additional lyrics*

If on-ly just to lift you up and rise a-bove the grey.

It breaks my heart but now you know that the bro-ken binds

are an o-pen door. And if it all dis-ap-pears,

I prom-ise you I'll still be there. 2. My But if the world

Chorus:

should let you down, if the sky should fall and nev-er make a sound.

I'll Still Be There - 3 - 1

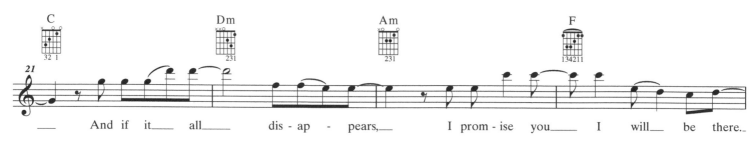

And if it___ all___ dis - ap - pears,___ I prom - ise you___ I will___ be there.__

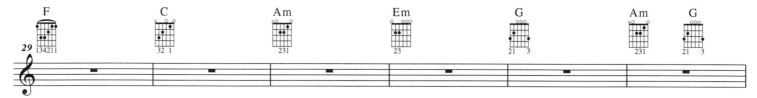

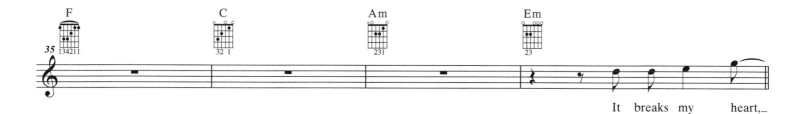

Rhy. Fig. 1
Elec. Gtr.

end Rhy. Fig. 1

Instrumental:

It breaks my heart,__

__ it breaks my heart,_____ it breaks my heart,__ it breaks my heart.___ But now you__ know__

Verse 3:

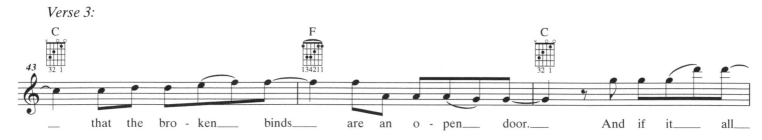

__ that the bro - ken___ binds___ are an o - pen__ door.___ And if it___ all___

Verse 2:
My growing pains, my darkest days, I owe them all to you.
For every break, I've got you to thank for always pulling me through.
If it breaks your heart, at least you know that the broken binds are an open door.
And if it all disappears, I promise you I'll still be there.
(To Chorus:)

WHAT DID I EVER COME HERE FOR

Moderately slow ♩ = 80

Words and Music by
PHIL HANSEROTH

*Recording sounds one whole step higher than written due to capo..
TAB numbers and chord frames relative to capo.

Verses 1 & 3:

1. I'd been gone___ for so___ long, and how I missed___ you,_____
3. *See additional lyrics*

___ my heart was ach - ing for home.

And then one___ day___ as I___ lay down,___ some - where far___ from you,

I dreamt that I heard you call my name, but my mind was play - ing games.

I knew right___ then___ that I'd___ re - turn to where I was___ be - fore.

And I was so tired of be - ing a - way that I just could - n't stay___ an - y - more.___

What Did I Ever Come Here For - 3 - 1

Instrumental:

D.S. % al Coda

⊕ *Coda*

What did I ev - er come__ here for. Oh, no,__

__ no, no,__ no, no,__ oh.__ What did I ev - er come__ here

for. Oh, no,__ no, no,__ no, no.__

Freely

__ What did I ev - er come__ here for.

Verse 3:

It wasn't too long before
I showed up at your door.
I'd been gone 1,000 miles,
I didn't know how much more I could stand,
If I could stand at all.
You said I looked like I'd been through World War II,
And my soul was worn right through.
I thought you would read my mind,
I thought you'd ask me to stay.

You never turn me away like before,
But you closed your door anyway.
What did I ever come here for.
Oh, no, no, no, no, oh.
What did I ever come here for.
Oh, no, no, no, no, oh.
What did I ever come here for.
Oh, no, no, no, no, oh.
What did I ever come here for.

HEART'S CONTENT

Words and Music by
BRANDI CARLILE

Moderately ♩ = 112

*Recording sounds four whole steps higher than written due to capo.
TAB numbers and chord frames relative to capo.

Verse 1:

May-be you thought I hung the moon,__ and may-be you__ thought we were John-ny and June.__

May - be we thought it was just us two, may - be we spoke too soon.____

Verses 2 & 3:

2. We nev - er lie and we don't tell tales,__ we bite our tongues and our fin - ger - nails.__
3. *See additional lyrics

We fall in love and we don't fall out, may - be we speak too soon.____

Chorus:

Here's to you and me____ and in - be - tween.__ We draw a line____ but we__ can't

Heart's Content - 3 - 1

Chorus:

Verse 3:
Maybe we hurt who we love the most,
Maybe it's all we can stand.
Maybe we walk through the world as ghosts,
Break my own heart before you can.
(To Chorus:)

RISE AGAIN

Words and Music by
TIM HANSEROTH, BRANDI CARLILE
and PHIL HANSEROTH

*Recording sounds four and 1/2 steps higher than written due to capo.
TAB numbers and chord frames relative to capo.

Rise Again - 3 - 1

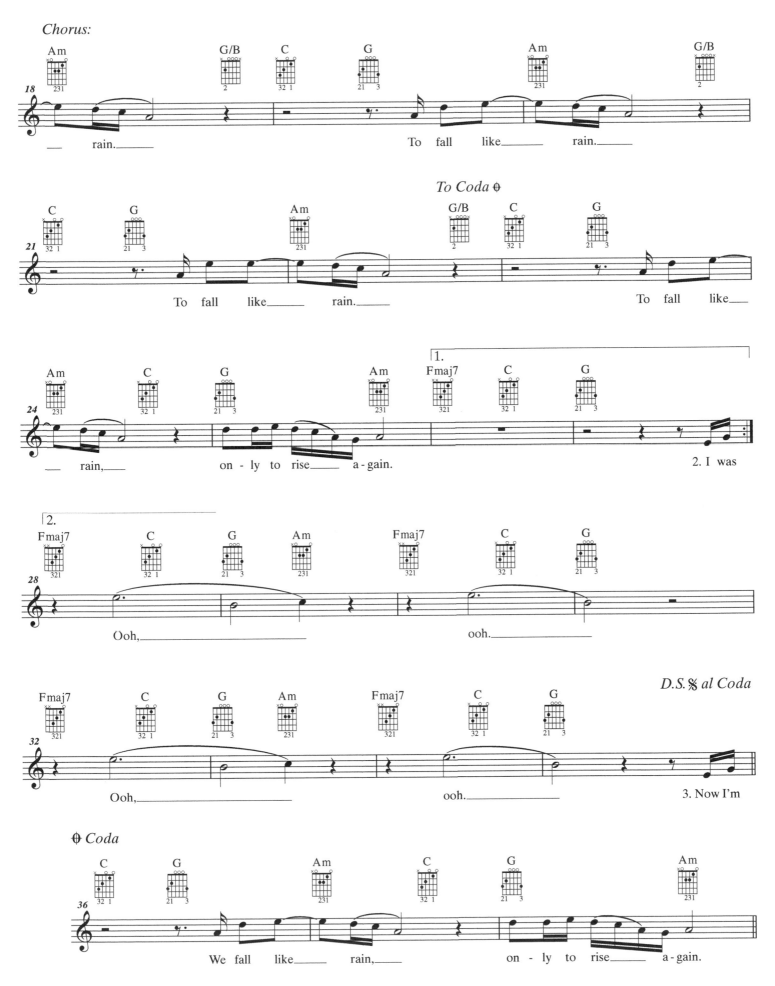

Interlude:

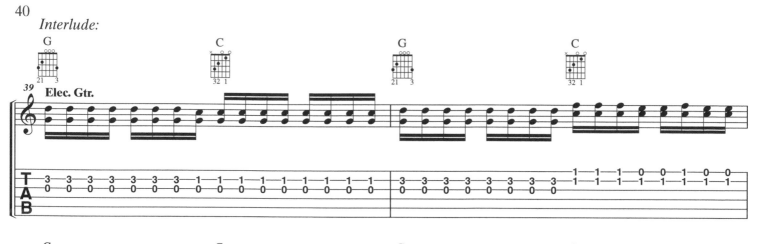

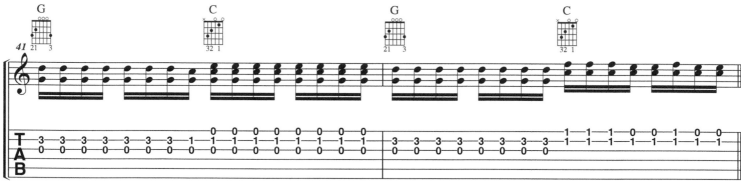

Outro:

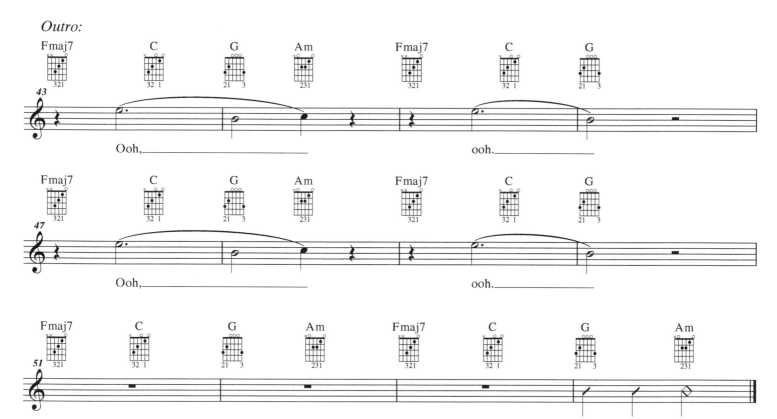

Ooh,_____ ooh._____

Ooh,_____ ooh._____

Verse 2:
I was longing for the wind when the trees begin to sway,
But I never grow my wings, no, I never fly away.
For the anchor of my love to which my heart is bound,
Is the iron for the cage that keeps me on the ground
To fall like rain.
(To Chorus:)

Verse 3:
Now I'm dreaming to myself with a tear behind my eye,
For a shelter is my mind in the quiet of the night.
Ever turning are the seasons,
Ever fading are the days,
And if there ever was a reason,
I just haven't found a way
To fall like rain.
(To Chorus:)

IN THE MORROW

Moderately slow ♩ = 86

Words and Music by
TIM HANSEROTH and BRANDI CARLILE

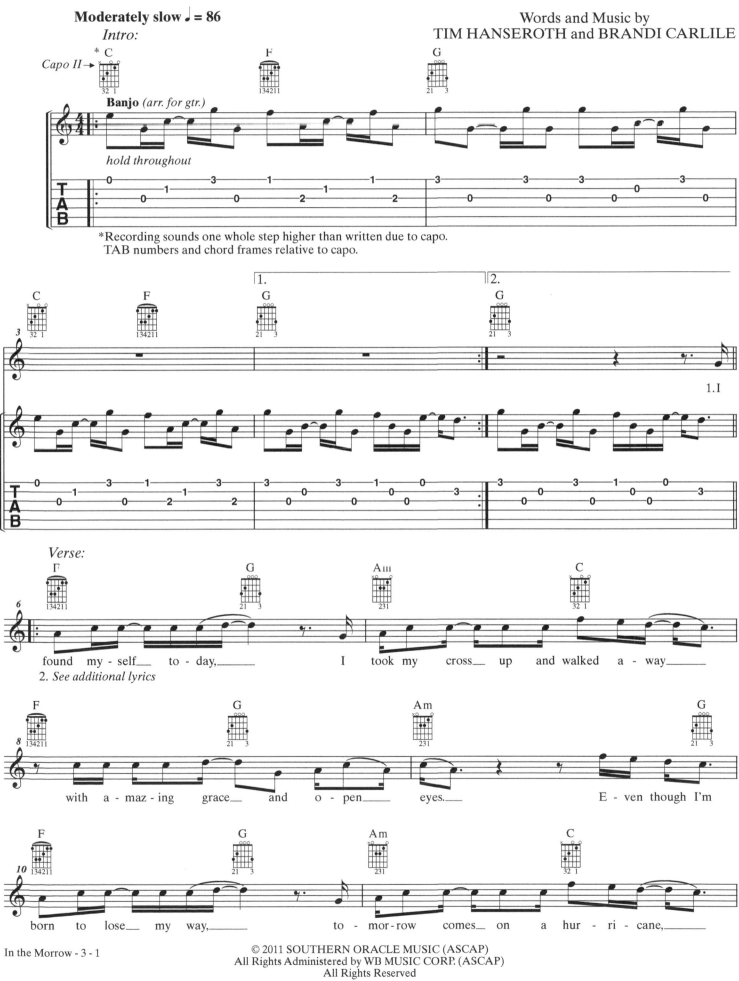

*Recording sounds one whole step higher than written due to capo.
TAB numbers and chord frames relative to capo.

Verse:

found my-self___ to-day,___ I took my cross___ up and walked a-way___

2. *See additional lyrics*

with a-maz-ing grace___ and o-pen___ eyes.___ E-ven though I'm

born to lose___ my way,___ to-mor-row comes___ on a hur-ri-cane,___

In the Morrow - 3 - 1

Verse 2:
No one sees it coming,
And no one walks when they should've been running,
Nothing hurts like knowing you tried.
And we can see how years can slip away
In the cold dark nights and the long hard days,
But nothing aches quite like goodbye.
(To Chorus:)

JUST KIDS

Moderately slow ♩ = 70

Intro:

Words and Music by
BRANDI CARLILE

1. Were we just___

Verses 1 & 2:

___ kids   just act-ing out?   Did-n't we know then___ what   love   was___ a - bout?___

(2.) *See additional lyrics*

_____   Were we just fool - ing,_____   play-ing a - round?   Were we ev - er

gon - na___ get   out   of___ this   town?_____   Move to Se - at - tle,___   stay up all___

___ night,   that was when bed - time___ was   our   big - gest   fight._____   Hoo,___

hoo,_____ hoo._____ Hoo,_

hoo,_____ hoo._____ 2. All in a ___ O - ver the

Verse 3:

rain - bow,_____ out in the snow, learn-ing to walk with__ the sand in__ our

toes._____ Long to be tall, kissed when you fall, hop-ing that

some - one__ will come when__ you call._____ You

Outro:

call,_____ you call,_____ you call._____

You ___ rit. ___ You ___

Verse 2:
All in a moment, all in a sound,
All in a day's work, we're tumbling down.
Down by the old school, trash in the street,
Searching the eyes of the strangers we meet.
Asking will it get better, will we be alone
Turning the wheels of our bicycles home.
(To Verse 3:)

GUITAR TAB GLOSSARY

TABLATURE EXPLANATION
TAB illustrates the six strings of the guitar.
Notes and chords are indicated by the placement of fret numbers on each string.

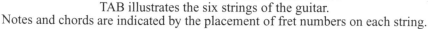
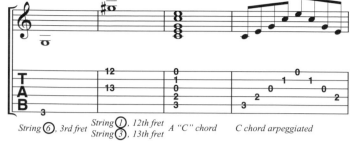

String ⑥, 3rd fret   String ①, 12th fret   A "C" chord   C chord arpeggiated
             String ③, 13th fret

BENDING NOTES

Half Step:
Play the note and bend string one half step (one fret).

Whole Step:
Play the note and bend string one whole step (two frets).

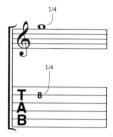

Slight Bend/ Quarter-Tone Bend:
Play the note and bend string sharp.

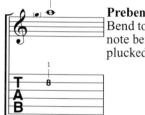

Prebend (Ghost Bend):
Bend to the specified note before the string is plucked.

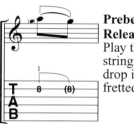

Prebend and Release:
Play the already-bent string, then immediately drop it down to the fretted note.

Unison Bend:
Play both notes and immediately bend the lower note to the same pitch as the higher note.

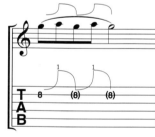

Bend and Release:
Play the note and bend to the next pitch, then release to the original note. Only the first note is attacked.

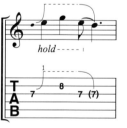

Bends Involving More Than One String:
Play the note and bend the string while playing an additional note on another string. Upon release, relieve the pressure from the additional note allowing the original note to sound alone.

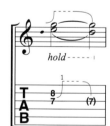

Bends Involving Stationary Notes:
Play both notes and immediately bend the lower note up to pitch. Release bend as indicated.

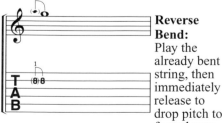

Reverse Bend:
Play the already bent string, then immediately release to drop pitch to fretted note.

Unison Bend:
Play both notes and immediately bend the lower note to the same pitch as the higher note.

Double Note Bend:
Play both notes and immediately bend both strings simultaneously up the indicated intervals.

ARTICULATIONS

Hammer On (Ascending Slur): Play the lower note, then "hammer" your finger to the higher note. Only the first note is plucked.

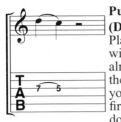

Pull Off (Descending Slur): Play the higher note with your first finger already in position on the lower note. Pull your finger off the first note with a strong downward motion that plucks the string—sounding the lower note.

Legato Slide: Play the first note and, keeping pressure applied on the string, slide up to the second note. The diagonal line shows that it is a slide and not a hammer-on or a pull-off.

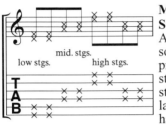

Muted Strings: A percussive sound is produced by striking the strings while laying the fret hand across them.

Palm Mute: The notes are muted (muffled) by placing the palm of the pick hand lightly on the strings, just in front of the bridge.

Left Hand Hammer: Using only the left hand, hammer on the first note played on each string.

Glissando: Play note and slide in specified direction.

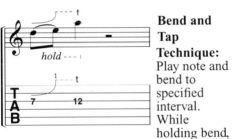

Bend and Tap Technique: Play note and bend to specified interval. While holding bend, tap onto fret indicated with a "t."

Fretboard Tapping: Tap onto the note indicated by the "t" with a finger of the pick hand, then pull off to the following note held by the fret hand.

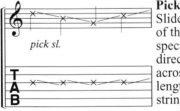

Pick Slide: Slide the edge of the pick in specified direction across the length of the strings.

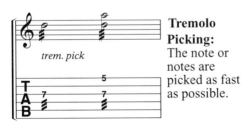

Tremolo Picking: The note or notes are picked as fast as possible.

Trill: Hammer on and pull off consecutively and as fast as possible between the original note and the grace note.

Vibrato: The pitch of a note is varied by a rapid shaking of the fret-hand finger, wrist, and forearm.

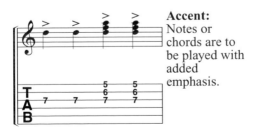

Accent: Notes or chords are to be played with added emphasis.

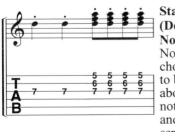

Staccato (Detached Notes): Notes or chords are to be played about half their noted value and with separation.

HARMONICS

Natural Harmonic:
A finger of the fret hand lightly touches the string at the note indicated in the TAB and is plucked by the pick producing a bell-like sound called a harmonic.

Artificial Harmonic:
Fret the note at the first TAB number, lightly touch the string at the fret indicated in parens (usually 12 frets higher than the fretted note), then pluck the string with an available finger or your pick.

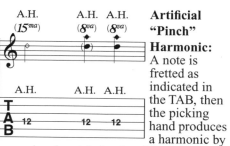

Artificial "Pinch" Harmonic:
A note is fretted as indicated in the TAB, then the picking hand produces a harmonic by squeezing the pick firmly while using the tip of the index finger in the pick attack. If parenthesis are found around the fretted note, it does not sound. No parenthesis means both the fretted note and the A.H. are heard simultaneously.

RHYTHM SLASHES

Strum Marks/ Rhythm Slashes:
Strum with the indicated rhythm pattern. Strum marks can be located above the staff or within the staff.

Single Notes with Rhythm Slashes:
Sometimes single notes are incorporated into a strum pattern. The circled number below is the string and the fret number is above.

TREMOLO BAR

Specified Interval:
The pitch of a note or chord is lowered to the specified interval and then return as indicated. The action of the tremolo bar is graphically represented by the peaks and valleys of the diagram.

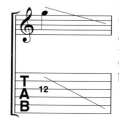

Unspecified Interval:
The pitch of a note or chord is lowered, usually very dramatically, until the pitch of the string becomes indeterminate.

PICK DIRECTION

Downstrokes and Upstrokes:
The downstroke is indicated with this symbol (⊓) and the upstroke is indicated with this (∨).